Georgia O'Keeffe

by Linda Lowery
illustrations by Rochelle Draper

Carolrhoda Books, Inc./Minneapolis

This book is available in two editions:
Library binding by Carolrhoda Books, Inc.
Soft cover by First Avenue Editions
Carolrhoda Books, Inc., and First Avenue Editions
c/o The Lerner Group
241 First Avenue North
Minneapolis, Minnesota 55401

Library of Congress Cataloging-in-Publication Data

Lowery, Linda.
  Georgia O'Keeffe / by Linda Lowery ; illustrations by
Rochelle Draper.
    p. cm.—(Carolrhoda on my own books)
  ISBN 0-87614-860-7 (lib. bdg.)
  ISBN 0-87614-898-4 (pbk.)
  1. O'Keeffe, Georgia, 1887–1986—Juvenile literature.
2. Painters—United States—Biography—Juvenile literature.
[1. O'Keeffe, Georgia, 1887–1986. 2. Artists. 3. Women—
Biography.] I. Draper, Rochelle, 1960–   ill. II. Title.
III. Series.
ND237.O5L68 1996
759.13—dc20   94-25413
[B]   CIP
                                             AC

Manufactured in the United States of America
1 2 3 4 5 6 I/SP 01 00 99 98 97 96

New Mexico
August 1930

Georgia O'Keeffe held the bone
up high.
She peered through the hole
in the middle.
Above was the endless blue sky
of New Mexico.
Below lay the soft red desert.
It was the most beautiful landscape
she had ever seen.

Georgia's trip was almost over.
She was thinking of bringing
some bones back to New York
to paint.
She chuckled to herself.
Whenever she painted
something new and different,
she confused people.
Some people would certainly complain
about painting bones.

After all, who ever thought
cow bones would make
beautiful pictures?
Nobody.
But Georgia often painted things
nobody else had ever thought
of painting.

*South Carolina
October 1915*

Fifteen years before,
Georgia's paintings
were not so unusual.
She was 27 years old,
and she lived in South Carolina.
In the mornings, she taught
art classes at Columbia College.

In the afternoons and evenings,
she painted.
Georgia hoped to be
an artist someday.
She worked hard at her painting.
But lately, it had not
been going well.

9

One October day,
Georgia took a long walk
in the woods.
Then she went straight to her studio.
She locked the door behind her.
She set out
all her drawings and paintings.
Squinting her eyes,
she looked at them one by one.

She noticed that this painting
was made to please a teacher.
That one she did for
an artist friend.
Other paintings looked just like
the work of famous European artists.
Not one painting was simply hers.
She had no idea
how to paint like Georgia O'Keeffe.

If she were to paint
just like herself,
and not like anyone else,
what would the painting look like?
Would it be tiny,
so people would have to look very
close to see what was in it?
Would it be huge,
so she would need a ladder
to reach the top?

Would it have perfect details,
like a photograph?
Or would it be abstract,
made of bold strokes
and colorful shapes?

For a long time,
Georgia looked and thought.
Ever since she was little,
shapes had floated in and out
of her mind.
She had imagined circles
and wavy forms.
Or tall lines that grew fat,
then skinny.

14

These shapes were not something
she had learned in school.
They were just things she imagined.
She had never thought
of putting them on paper.
They were not the kinds of things
painters were supposed to paint.

15

There and then,
Georgia made up her mind.
If these odd shapes
were what she saw,
then these odd shapes
were exactly what she would paint.

Georgia rushed off a letter
to her best friend,
Anita Pollitzer,
who lived in New York.
"I'm starting all over new,"
she wrote.

Georgia stashed her old paintings
in a closet.
She packed up her paints
and her brushes.
She bought big, white paper
for drawing.
She pulled out
her black charcoal sticks.
Then she sat on the floor
with her paper taped
to the closet door.

Georgia drew a curve that rose high,
then drooped over
at the top of the page.
She drew a thin line that grew thick
in the middle,
and then thin again.
It looked like an opening in the sky.
She drew spirals spinning down.
She drew waves reaching up.
One night,
Georgia had a bad headache.

"Well, why not do something with it?"
she thought.
So she drew a picture
of how the pain felt,
pounding in her head.

Night after night, Georgia worked
until the charcoal crumbled
in her hand.
Her fingers got so sore
she could hardly hold a pen
to write to Anita.
"Am I completely mad?" she wrote.
She wondered if
drawing such strange shapes
meant she was insane.
Maybe this was not art at all.
Maybe it was just crazy scribbles.
"Keep at it," Anita wrote back.

Once during Christmas break,
Georgia stayed up all night working.
When the sun came up,
she crawled into bed.
She had many drawings now.
It was time to show them to someone.

23

On New Year's Day, 1916, Anita
received a package in the mail.
It was a roll of drawings.
Anita took the package into a room
and locked the door.
She lay the drawings all around her.

What wild shapes
her friend Georgia had made!
They were only black marks on paper.
But they seemed to
jump and crash and flow.
They split open.
They spilled over.
To Anita, the drawings looked alive.
She stared at them for an hour.

Then Anita remembered
she had tickets to see *Peter Pan*.
She didn't want to go
without Georgia's drawings.
So she tucked them under her arm
and went off to the theater.
All through the play,
she held Georgia's drawings close.

When Anita left the theater,
she hurried through
the dark, rainy streets.
She went right to
Alfred Stieglitz's gallery.

Anita and Georgia had been
to the gallery many times
with their classmates.
They had had long, lively talks with
Mr. Stieglitz about the pictures
that hung there.
He showed modern art
by new artists such as Picasso,
Matisse, and Rodin.

Anita's heart beat fast.
She was a little afraid
of Mr. Stieglitz.
With his long, black cape
and bushy mustache,
he was very dramatic.
Sometimes he could also be rude.
But what if he liked these drawings?
It would mean that Georgia's work
was as good as Anita thought it was.

29

Anita pushed the elevator button,
but the elevator was broken.
She found the stairs,
climbed up four floors,
and burst in on Mr. Stieglitz.
She ignored his grumpy glare.
She had to do this for Georgia.

"Would you like to see what I have
under my arm?" Anita asked.
Mr. Stieglitz told her
to spread the drawings on the floor.
He fingered his round, wire glasses.
He stared quietly for a long time.
Finally, he spoke.

Mr. Stieglitz told Anita that
the drawings were not like anything
he had ever seen.
He could see that Georgia O'Keeffe
had been true to herself.
Her heart and soul
showed in the drawings.
He said he could see
"a woman on paper."
"I wouldn't mind showing these
sometime," he told Anita.

Alfred Stieglitz
hung the drawings in his gallery
that very spring, in 1916.
They made a big stir.
Some people loved them.
Others called them "strange"
and "shocking."
So many people came to see them
that the pictures stayed up
for two extra months.

Georgia grew to know Alfred very well
after that.
Alfred was a photographer,
using his camera
to make beautiful pictures.
Often, Georgia and Alfred
made pictures of the same things.
In 1920,
Georgia began painting apples.
"She has apple fever,"
Alfred explained.
The next year,
Alfred took photographs of apples.

When Alfred photographed skies,
Georgia painted skies.
They both made pictures of barns
and the house where they spent
their summers.
Together, they made a great team,
and in 1924, they were married.

Georgia went on to paint
hundreds more pictures.
She painted the tall sparkling
buildings of New York.

She painted colorful flowers
that were so big
people felt as if
they were climbing inside.

New Mexico
August 1930

When she visited New Mexico,
Georgia began to think
about painting bones.
She turned the bone over and over in
her hand.
To her, it was precious.
"I have wanted to paint the desert,
and I haven't known how,"
she thought.

Now, deep inside, she did know how.

White bones and blue sky.

White bones and red hills.

White bones and clouds.

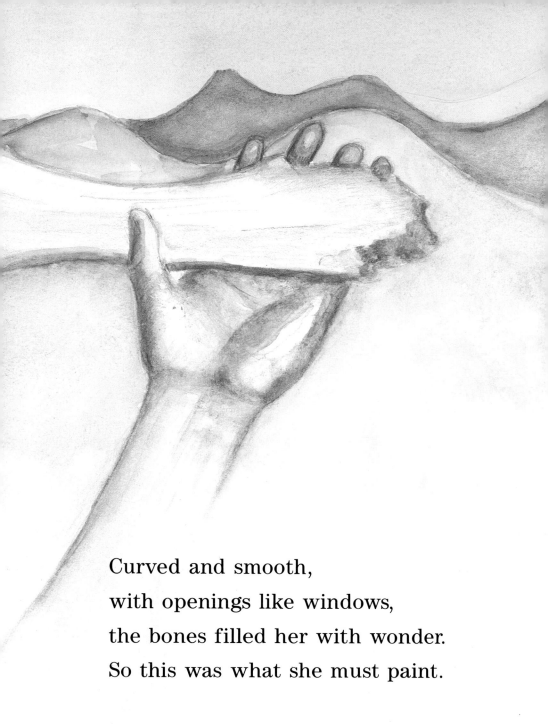

Curved and smooth,
with openings like windows,
the bones filled her with wonder.
So this was what she must paint.

She turned her back
on the bright New Mexico sun
and headed inside.
She gathered all the bones
she had collected.
Carefully, she packed them up
in a big, wooden barrel.
Then she shipped the barrel
to New York.

When Alfred went to pick up
the barrel,
he had to pay for the shipping.
It was so heavy,
it cost him sixteen dollars.
"That's a lot of money to pay for
some old bones!" he complained.

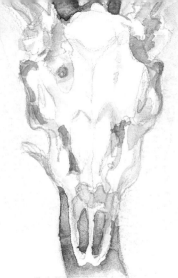

When Georgia got back and showed
Alfred her first bone painting,
he laughed.
"What do you expect to do with that?"
he asked.
Some people agreed with Alfred.
They thought painting bones
was a spooky idea.
But many people found the paintings
beautiful.
They appeared in magazines.
They were sold to famous museums.

Georgia painted bones for many years.
And when she grew tired
of painting bones,
what did she paint then?
Georgia O'Keeffe painted
whatever pleased her,
no matter what
the rest of the world thought.

Afterword

Each spring after 1931, Georgia set out from New York with tubes of paint and rolls of canvas. She drove her shiny black Model A Ford into the New Mexico desert. When she found a scene that made her happy, she took out her supplies and painted. Every autumn she returned to New York, her car loaded down with paintings for Alfred to show the world.

Alfred died in 1946, and Georgia moved to Abiquiú (AB-ee-cue), New Mexico. To her, it was "the most wonderful place in the world." Museums bought her paintings, and she won many prizes for her work.

Until the age of 98, Georgia kept on painting whatever she saw, exactly the way she saw it. It did not matter what anyone thought. Each painting was hers—a genuine Georgia O'Keeffe.

Important Dates

November 15, 1887—Born in Sun Prairie, Wisconsin
1902—Family moved to Williamsburg, Virginia
1905–1908—Studied art in Chicago and New York
1916—First major exhibit, at Alfred Stieglitz's 291
     Gallery
1918—Began painting full-time; moved to New York
1918–1932—Created most of her flower paintings
1924—Married Alfred Stieglitz
1929—First summer in Taos, New Mexico
1930—Began painting bones
1946—Alfred died
1949—Moved permanently to Abiquiú, New Mexico
1977—Received Medal of Freedom from U. S.
     government
1985—Received National Medal of Arts
March 6, 1986—Died in Santa Fe, New Mexico, at
     age 98